Nipper

Written by
Daisy Hawkins

Illustrated by
Kevin Hopgood

ransom

Back in 1981 ...
We need this wedding on TV for all to see.
2

Yes, but the TV cord needs to go under the road. And to go under the road, the TV cord has to go in that tunnel.
That is not a tunnel!
This is not good.

Wait! An animal might fit! Nipper might fit!

In a garden not far-off ...
I need you, Nipper. We all need you.

Back at the tunnel ...
This is madness. Pure madness.
Um, is that rat up to the job?

Nipper is a ferret, Ben, not a rat. And she **is** up to it.
Let me get her secure in her harness. Then we can add the TV cord.

The cord is light and food will lure her down the tunnel. She will be quick if we meet her with this.
OK, I am in. I will man this bit. You go and meet her with the food.
Shall I inform the queen that a ferret is on the job?

8

Let her go!
Go on, Nipper!
For king and queen!

You did it, Nipper. Now all of us can see the big wedding.
All hail to the rat!

Nipper the ferret, 1981